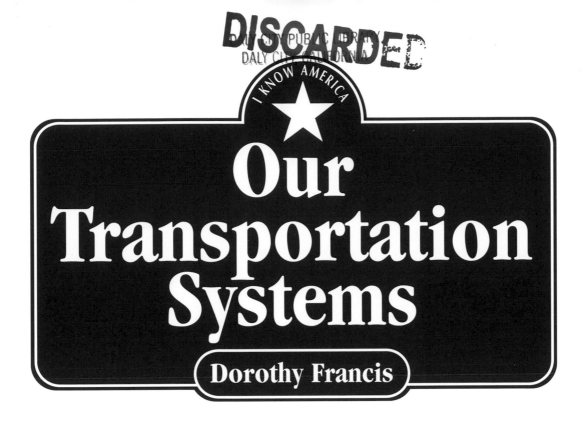

I KNOW AMERICA

Our Transportation Systems

Dorothy Francis

THE MILLBROOK PRESS
Brookfield, Connecticut

W

Cover photograph courtesy of GALA/SuperStock

Photographs courtesy of PhotoEdit, Inc.: p. 4 (© David Young-Wolff); North Wind Picture Archives: pp. 6, 7, 12, 15, 33; Liaison Agency/Hulton Getty: pp. 8, 20, 30, 35; Library of Congress: pp. 10 (LC-D420-2659), 11 (LC-USZC4-4427), 27; Culver Pictures, Inc.: p. 17; FPG International: p. 18 (© 1997 Ron Chapple); Utah State Historical Society: pp. 22, 25; Amtrak: p. 28; DVIC: p. 36 (PH2 August Sigur); SuperStock: pp. 37 (© Malcolm Fife), 43 (© Kevin Moan); The Granger Collection, New York: p. 38; Archive Photos: p. 41; NASA: p. 44.

Library of Congress Cataloging-in-Publication Data
Francis, Dorothy.
Our transportation systems / Dorothy Francis.
p. cm. – (I know America)
Includes bibliographical references and index.
ISBN 0-7613-2366-X (lib. bdg.)
1. Transportation—United States—Juvenile literature. 2. Transportation—United States—History—Juvenile literature. [1. Transportation. 2. Transportation—History.]
I. Title. II. Series.
HE203 .F7 2002 388'.0973—dc21
2001030883

Published by The Millbrook Press, Inc.
2 Old New Milford Road
Brookfield, Connecticut 06804
www.millbrookpress.com

CONTENTS

CHAPTER

GETTING FROM HERE TO THERE

Every day you or someone you know needs to travel somewhere.

Do you need a ride to a friend's house or to school? Do your parents drive to work? Did your sister take a train to college? Did a military ship bring your brother home from abroad? Are your grandparents flying to visit you? People need to get from here to there. Also, people need to move produce and manufactured goods by land, sea, and air to places where those things are needed.

The Department of Transportation (DOT), a branch of our federal government, regulates travel in America. Its job is to promote safe and efficient travel. A secretary who is appointed by the president manages the DOT.

In colonial days, Americans either walked or rode on horseback. They also used the kinds of horse-drawn carts and stagecoaches some of them had known in Europe. Carts could carry only one or two people, but stagecoaches could carry six or eight. The

Whether it's by family car or jumbo jet, people need to get from place to place every day. Transportation is important to our economy, too, because it is used to ship goods all around the country.

5

This picture of a stagecoach was made in 1795.

coaches stopped at "stages" where passengers boarded and where the drivers changed horses. Every ten miles they needed fresh horses in order to maintain speed. Armed guards rode each stagecoach because robbers were a constant danger.

But the time arrived when carriages and stagecoaches no longer met the needs of the people.

WESTWARD HO!

By 1830, many Americans who could not find jobs headed west to seek their fortunes. These pioneers traveled in covered wagons called Conestogas. They nicknamed their wagons "prairie schooners" because the wagon covers reminded them of ship sails. Ox teams pulled these wagons, which weighed more than a ton and could carry four tons of cargo.

Heading into unknown territory, the pioneers formed convoys of twenty or more wagons. They faced bad weather, breakdowns, and diseases such as cholera and smallpox. Occasionally they had to defend themselves against attacks by Native Americans. Perhaps they sometimes envied their friends who had stayed behind.

Conestoga wagons were sometimes called "prairie schooners" because their white covers reminded people of the sails on a type of sailing ship called a schooner.

In the late 1860s, the idea of a two-wheeled bicycle spread from Europe to America. The first bicycles had no steering. The rider sat on the seat, pushing and guiding the wheels with the feet. Later, handlebars and pedals were added. As the years went by bicycles grew in popularity. People chose bicycles not only for transportation, but also for exercise and for fun. Today's manufacturers produce multispeed bicycles. Riders choose them for recreation and for racing. America's racing success in the 1984 Olympic Games gave bicycles new popularity. Mountain bike racing, included in the 1996 Olympics, increased that popularity.

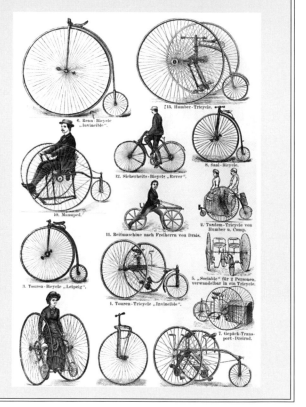

BUGGIES, BUSES, AND TRAMS

People who remained in the East invented a two-wheeled, covered buggy. One or two people traveling a short distance found the one-horse shay suitable.

Workers living in cities needed rides to their jobs, so they developed horse-drawn buses and trolleys. In 1826, Gridley Bryant built America's first horse-drawn train. It rolled slowly along a three-mile railroad carrying granite to a construction site.

People eventually needed a means of city travel that would be faster than the horse-drawn buses or trolleys. The invention of the electric generator in the

1870s provided it. The electric generator allowed electricity to travel through wires. German engineer Ernst Werner Von Siemens devised an electric overhead-wire system for powering streetcars. People could then travel with no need for horses. But before long something even more amazing was being developed.

THE HORSELESS CARRIAGE

Inventors built a machine that used the steam from boiling water to make power. These steam engines could propel carriages, but boiler explosions made such carriages dangerous. The invention of the internal combustion engine made a horseless vehicle, the automobile, a reality. Gasoline burning *within* the engine powered these vehicles. Travelers no longer needed horses or steam engines.

The automobile has had a tremendous impact on people's lives. Cars required tires, gasoline, and engine and body parts. Many industries developed to supply those needs. Poverty decreased when people found new jobs in the automobile industry.

Many carmakers became well known. Ford, Cadillac, Packard, Oldsmobile, and Buick are just a few. But to many Americans, the word "car" meant "Ford." More than 15 million Model T Fords had been built when American production of this model stopped in 1927.

Once motor cars became common, motor buses soon followed. By the 1930s, the electric streetcars and their tracks began to disappear from city streets.

Meanwhile, Americans had fallen in love with the automobile, and concerns about it and its future remain with us today.

As a farm boy, Henry Ford liked to tinker with engines. His tinkering developed into a lifelong career. In 1896, Henry worked as an engineer in Detroit. At home in his spare time, he built an automobile. That automobile's success allowed Henry to quit his job and devote all of his time to building cars.

Henry believed that outstanding speed would set his car apart from others that had been developed. He was right. In 1902, his car beat the foremost racing car, the Winton Bullet, by half a mile. Wealthy men noticed Henry's car and they backed him with money. At last he could build his dream car.

Ford's first company failed after making only twenty cars. However, he didn't give up. He and his backers established the Ford Motor Company. Henry served as its vice president and manager.

Ford believed that Americans wanted an inexpensive, reliable car. On August 12, 1908, the Ford Motor Company provided that car: the Model T. This two-seater was noted for being easy to build and easy to repair. It cost $850, and people nicknamed it the Tin Lizzie.

When Model T production stopped in 1927, the car cost only $250. It was the last of America's early cars. It was the first of America's modern cars.

In 1924, Henry Ford posed with the first automobile he built (right) and a Model T. On the door of the Model T is painted "The Ten Millionth Ford."

THE FUTURE OF THE AUTOMOBILE

In 1927, there were only about 15 million automobiles on American roads. Nobody worried about fuel shortages or polluted air.

Today, about 400 million cars of various kinds exist. It is estimated that by the year 2030 there will be one billion cars in the world. Their energy use will increase air pollution. Carmakers and oil companies continue to seek ways to cut pollution levels.

Right now the only type of vehicle that is completely pollution-free is the battery-powered electric car. Experiments with these vehicles continue.

Some people believe that pollution will strip our planet of its resources. Others believe that scientists will solve pollution problems. They believe that future cars will be better than ever; cleaner, safer, and more beautiful.

Let's hope these people are right!

The 1955 Studebaker Commander V-8 Regal
Conestoga Station Wagon
FOR SIX PASSENGERS

By the 1950s, most American families owned one or two cars and drove almost everywhere they went. This 1955 car is called the "Conestoga station wagon," referring to the popular type of transportation from a hundred years earlier.

CHAPTER

2

ROADS

Americans have always needed roads.

Colonists often used trails made by Native Americans. Those people had followed animal paths that led to water. Some of the roads you use today may at one time have been paths worn smooth by hairy mammoths, bison, or bears.

CONESTOGA TRAILS

Pioneers in Conestoga wagons blazed trails leading west. They crossed deserts and mountains. They forded rivers and streams. They traveled in all kinds of weather.

At dusk, Conestoga drivers circled their wagons. They chained each wagon tongue to the rear axle of the wagon ahead. The wagons formed a corral for the animals and a fort against enemies.

Pioneers sometimes had to lighten their loads so their oxen could keep up with the rest. Abandoned

In some places, like where this picture was taken in Wyoming, ruts worn into the sandstone from years of heavy wagons traveling the Oregon Trail can still be seen today.

THE CALF PATH by Sam Walter Foss

One day through the primeval wood
A calf walked home, as good calves should;
But he made a trail all bent askew,
A crooked trail, as all calves do . . .
This forest trail became a lane
That bent and turned and turned again.
And this, before men were aware,
Became a city's crowded thoroughfare . . .
And men two centuries and a half
Trod in the footsteps of that calf.

furniture, clothing, and dishes littered the Oregon and Santa Fe trails for many years. In some places, ruts left by Conestoga wheels can still be seen.

THE DEMAND FOR BETTER ROADS

In the 1880s, bicyclists began demanding better roads. Nobody listened. Twenty years later, bicyclists and car drivers still faced dangerous roads. Brick or pavement sometimes covered city streets, but most country roads were dirt paths. In warm months, they were dry and dusty or wet and muddy. In winter, they could be covered with ice or snow. Most roads were so narrow that, if two cars met, one might be forced into a ditch along the side of the road.

Hitting a hole in the road could cause a bicyclist to crash or a car driver to break an axle. Travelers also had to guard against sharp stones that punctured tires. Drivers considered it a great feat to cover fifty miles in one day.

In 1904, there were about two million miles of public highway. Gravel covered about 100,000 of those miles. Macadam, a mixture of crushed rock and tar, covered another 40,000. The rest were dirt.

THE AMERICAN AUTOMOBILE ASSOCIATION

In 1904, people interested in travel organized the American Automobile Association (AAA). The group had two goals. The first goal was to help travelers in

Even the rugged four-wheel-drive vehicles of today would have trouble driving on this 1908 street! In the early twentieth century, many roads and city streets were as poor as this one.

15

trouble. The second goal was to point out America's need for better roads. To reach these goals, the AAA sponsored a driving tour from New York through New England and back. They named it the Glidden Tour after Charles Glidden, who contributed the winner's trophy.

In the Glidden tour, speed did not count. Judges awarded points on the basis of a car's performance. Drivers entering the best-known cars in America drove through mud, rain, and dust. They urged their cars up steep hills and across rickety bridges. Unlucky drivers faced ruined tires and broken axles. Due to bad road conditions, drivers sometimes crashed into each other.

The Pierce Great Arrow won the tour. But the attention that the tour brought to the state of America's roads was far more important than the name of the winner.

CONGRESS TAKES ACTION

Lawmakers began to listen to people's demands for better roads. In 1916, Congress passed the Federal Aid Road Act. This law gave financial help to America's road system, and roads began to improve.

World War II made Americans realize that our nation needed better roads to move troops and war equipment from coast to coast. In 1944, Congress approved the Interstate Highway System. It was the largest public works program in history.

The new superhighways built as a result of the creation of the Interstate Highway System were at least four lanes wide, with the lanes for cars heading

in one direction separated from the lanes heading in the other direction. These new highways increased America's economic growth by allowing people to move produce and manufactured goods to market more easily. The superhighways also reduced traffic injuries. And they increased America's defense capabilities by making it easier to transport troops and military supplies. Americans paid for their superhighways through taxes and toll fees.

Large-scale highway building began soon after approval of the Interstate Highway System in 1944. This picture was taken during construction of the Pennsylvania Turnpike.

17

The NHS works to improve today's highways, which are so important to our daily lives and to the economy of the United States.

Twelve years later, President Dwight D. Eisenhower signed the Federal Aid Highway Act of 1956. That law authorized the building of over 40,000 miles of high-quality highway to tie the nation together. That highway system was completed in 1975.

After another two decades, the National Highway System Designation Act chose 160,955 miles of roads as the National Highway System (NHS). These NHS miles include the Interstate Highway System plus other roads important to America's economy, defense, and people's ability to move around.

The NHS is to be an important part of our national transportation network in the twenty-first century. It encourages states to improve their important highways by using federal funds. The NHS will help people get to work and to school, visit distant family and friends, and travel to new places. In addition, it will assure that our nation remains strong and prosperous by increasing our ability to compete in the worldwide marketplace.

RAILROADS

Railroading began in England. Engineer George Stephenson planned the first railway lines for self-propelled trains there in the early 1800s. The Delaware and Hudson Canal Company in New York brought a steam locomotive from England in 1829. Its sixteen-mile iron-track railway ran in New York and Pennsylvania. For the first time, wheels carried people faster than horses. This steam engine operated like the steam engines used in the early development of horseless carriages.

Unfortunately, the iron rails proved too brittle for pounding train wheels. But after Englishman Henry Bessemer perfected a method of making steel, steel rails surpassed iron rails in time for the railroad boom of the 1860s.

In this scene from 1830, a horse-drawn rail car races an early steam train, which was designed to replace it.

21

THE DREAM OF A TRANSCONTINENTAL RAILROAD

When train tracks reached from the Atlantic Coast to the Mississippi River, people dreamed of a coast-to-coast railroad. Such a line would promote business by transporting people and products across the nation.

Using private funds, owners of the Union Pacific Railroad built a railroad bridge across the Mississippi at Rock Island, Illinois. This angered steamboat owners. Steamboats were kings of the cargo transport

The labor of Chinese immigrants played an important part in the building of the Central Pacific Railroad. Chinese workers could be identified by the wide-brimmed hats they often wore.

business, and competition from trains was not welcome.

Soon after workers completed the railroad bridge, the steamboat *Effie Afton* hit a bridge support. As the bridge and boat burned, steamship captains cheered. The *Effie Afton*'s captain sued the railroad. He claimed that bridge supports created currents harmful to steamships.

The owners of the Union Pacific railroad hired a defense lawyer named Abraham Lincoln. Lincoln argued in favor of the railroads. He won his case, and railroad fever began to sweep the nation.

No matter how badly people wanted a transcontinental railroad, the Civil War slowed building plans. Even so, Leland Stanford, who later became California's governor, established the Central Pacific Railroad Company. After the war, Stanford's railroad in the West rivaled Thomas Durant's Union Pacific Railroad in the East.

Irish immigrants and freed slaves rushed to work for the Union Pacific, but the Central Pacific struggled to find workers. Gold-seeking drifters shunned the railroad's hard work and low pay. Instead, Stanford hired Chinese immigrants. Eventually, the Central Pacific employed almost every Chinese male in California.

THE RACE WAS ON

The two railway companies began a friendly competition to see which one could reach the Utah border first in the building of the transcontinental railroad. At the same time, a new era in America's history began—the Wild West.

So-called railroad towns with names like North Platte, Abilene, Cheyenne, Laramie, and Medicine Bend sprang up overnight to cater to the railroad workers' needs by selling food, supplies, and entertainment. Legends grew around the towns and their people.

The railroads needed meat to feed the workers, so they hired buffalo hunter William Cody. Today we still hear tales of Buffalo Bill. People in Abilene elected a fearsome mayor. Few outlaws wanted to tangle with the legendary Wild Bill Hickok.

As work continued, Union Pacific workers faced attack when they trespassed on Native American land. The Central Pacific avoided such problems. If Native Americans appeared, the railroad boss hired them. He needed every worker he could get.

THE GREAT PACIFIC RAILROAD IS COMPLETED

The Union Pacific crews crossed the Utah border first. Both companies agreed to meet at Promontory Point. On May 10, 1869, workers hoisted an American flag on a telegraph pole, a band played patriotic tunes, and a railroad official pounded in a golden spike that marked the completion of the transcontinental railroad.

Telegraph operators sped the news across America. The railroad race had ended. America was the true winner. And a new age of railroading began.

THE GOLDEN AGE OF RAILROADING

Historians call the period between 1869 and 1910 the Golden Age of Railroading. Other railroads

reached the Pacific coast during this time, such as the Atchison, Topeka & Santa Fe, and the Western Pacific. Smaller railroads connected to that mainline network.

Railroads had spanned great distances. Now passengers wanted speed. In 1893, the New York Central's Empire State Express recorded a run of 100 miles per hour. This pleased passengers, but for moving freight, a train's ability to carry great weight was more important to railroad owners than its speed. Cargo shipments brought in more money than passenger fares. Railroad companies developed powerful engines for moving goods.

The transcontinental railroad was completed when work crews from the Union Pacific and Central Pacific railroads met at Promontory Point, Utah, on May 10, 1869.

25

In the 1890s, German inventor Rudolf Diesel produced an engine that burned oil. By the 1930s in America, diesel engines began to replace steam engines. The *Zephyr,* owned by the Chicago, Burlington & Quincy Railroad, was America's first diesel train in regular service.

THE LUXURY OF RAILROAD TRAVEL

Railroads soon competed to provide passengers with luxuries. Each company tried to outdo the others in the use of electric lights, comfortable seats, and sleeping spaces. Passengers who didn't care to bring a lunch could eat in a dining car. There the wealthiest passengers found gleaming silver, elegant china, and fine food. For many years, people thought that traveling by train was *the* way to go.

AMTRAK

Although railway companies provided passengers with luxuries, passenger service gradually declined. Automobiles improved. Highways improved. Many people preferred to travel by car so they could create their own routes and time schedules. Cargo profits declined when business people began to show a preference for shipping their goods on trucks, ships, and airplanes. Railroad usage decreased greatly in the 1950s and 1960s.

To combat that decline in business, the Department of Transportation worked with railroad officials to create a passenger railway service called Amtrak in 1971. Now, in the twenty-first century,

Overnight travelers sometimes reserved Pullman sleeper cars. The Pullman car, designed by George Pullman, looked much like a regular day coach.

In 1857, the first Pullman cars had accommodations for ten sleepers, a washstand at each end, stove heating, oil lamps, and plush seats that could be made into beds. The upper berths were suspended from the ceiling by ropes and were hauled out of sight by day.

As years passed, Pullman cars were modernized. They could sleep twelve people and they had electric lights and a shower in each car. Travelers also could reserve individual sleeping compartments with a private sink, toilet, and bed. In private compartments, a cabin steward left a chocolate and the next day's itinerary on the traveler's pillow each night.

This railroad advertisement from 1910 aims to tell travelers about the luxury of its Pullman cars.

Amtrak operates a profitable, 22,000-mile, intercity rail system, serving forty-five states. Passengers have many choices of accommodations, from Deluxe, with private rooms, sofas, and armchairs that convert into beds, to Coach, where seats recline for sleeping.

In addition to Amtrak, many cities offer subway travel. Computers program these underground trains to operate without the need of station staff. People who work in crowded cities find subways an inexpensive and quick way to get around.

Also, some cities have commuter trains and overhead monorails that run above other traffic routes.

Such railways transport people swiftly to and from cities, relieving traffic on crowded streets.

In this new century, our nation's railroads continue an honorable tradition of service. They are a cornerstone of America's economy as they allow passengers and cargo to move from here to there quickly and efficiently.

CHAPTER

WATER TRAVEL

People had known for centuries that wind pushing against a sail would move a boat. Until the invention of the steam engine, wind power was the only alternative to muscle power.

Colonists built sailing ships for river, lake, and ocean travel. No water route connected the Atlantic Ocean and the Great Lakes, and merchants needed to move people and cargo faster between the two than overland routes allowed. In the early 1800s, imaginative thinkers suggested digging a waterway—a canal.

THE ERIE CANAL

Many people, including President Thomas Jefferson, scoffed at the idea. But New York's governor, DeWitt Clinton, convinced lawmakers to fund such a project. In 1817, crews of local laborers and untrained Irish immigrants began digging. They started at Rome, New York, working for a few cents an hour plus a daily quart of whiskey. And they built a canal.

The Erie Canal was important to the nation's economy in the early 1800s. This scene from Lockport, New York, shows one of the canal's locks and a railroad bridge spanning the canal in the distance.

31

Shipboard life wasn't for sissies. Voyages might last over a year. Ships carried little drinking water and no ice. They carried no canned foods, fresh vegetables, or fruit, so sailors sometimes became ill from the lack of proper nutrition.

A successful seaman, Captain Cook, understood the need for vegetables. His crews seldom suffered from scurvy, a disease common to sailors, because he carried vats of sauerkraut aboard ship.

The hardest work was rigging the sails. During storms, sailors climbed masts to adjust the sails while the ship tossed and turned. If they failed in their duties, sails could be shredded and the masts could break like matchsticks.

In addition to these hardships, sailors had no beds. They slept on the hard deck or in canvas hammocks.

In 1825, Governor Clinton poured a keg of Erie Canal water into New York Harbor. This marked the completion of the 363-mile canal. Towpaths along the edge of the canal allowed mules to pull floating barges at a rate of one mile per hour. Success! The Erie Canal linked the Great Lakes with the Hudson River and the Atlantic Ocean. It was the most successful of America's early canals.

SAILBOATS

While canals provided an efficient way to transport goods, few people wanted to travel by mule-drawn barge on a canal. Instead, many travelers looked to sailing ships for transportation. Sailing ships have two advantages over other ships. Wind power is free, and little space is required for spare sails and masts. The

Clipper ships, like the *Caribee*, built in Maine in 1852, were designed for speed.

33

disadvantage of sailing ships is their dependence on weather. Sometimes they must zigzag off course to catch needed breezes. And sometimes there are no breezes to catch.

Seamen used many kinds of sailboats. Whalers sailed long, narrow boats that could turn quickly to follow their prey. These boats required only one mast, sails, and harpoon lines. They also needed stoves for boiling whale fat, places to stow barrels of whale oil, and living quarters for crewmen. Whalers sometimes stayed at sea for years.

Schooners, called tall ships, had two or more masts and many sails. Fishermen used them for commercial fishing. Merchants sailed them to foreign shores to buy and sell wares. Wreckers, who saved people and cargo from sinking ships, used schooners as salvage boats. Pirates used schooners to prey on other ships.

Seamen used heavily armed and fast-moving frigates to defend America's shores. The most important sailing ship preserved in America is the USS *Constitution* in Boston Harbor. This frigate carried forty-four guns and protected our country in the War of 1812.

Merchants used three-masted clipper ships when speed was more vital than the ship's cargo capacity. America's long, narrow Yankee clippers were fastest of all.

STEAMSHIPS

The invention of the steam engine in the late 1700s didn't make sailboats obsolete. Steam engines replaced ships' wood-burning engines, and early

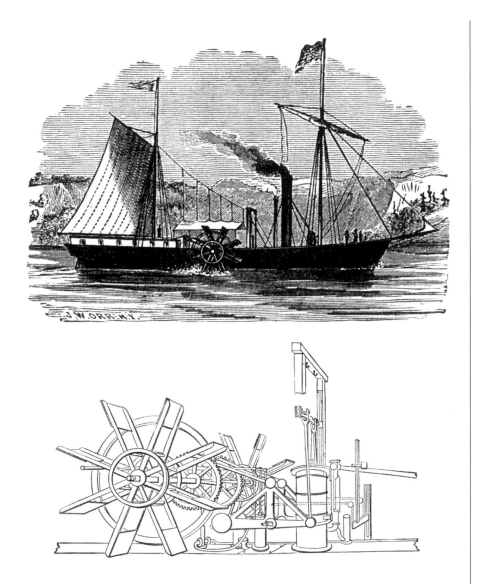

The steamship *Clermont*, built by Robert Fulton, is pictured here at left, along with a diagram of its paddle wheel (bottom).

steamboats used both sails and steam-powered paddle wheels to move a vessel from port to port. Because fuel was costly, ship captains sometimes used sails for economy. The *Clermont* was the first steamship to post a regular schedule along New York's Hudson River.

It was about 1900 before submarines, or underwater boats, could travel safely on diesel power. Many of today's submarines carry missiles for firing through tubes at the ship's top.

The partly submerged nuclear-powered submarine USS *Pasadena* moves out of Pearl Harbor, Hawaii, with its crew standing on top.

After World War II, gas turbines and diesel engines proved most efficient for powering steamships.

TWENTY-FIRST-CENTURY SHIPS

In the twenty-first century, oil tankers are the world's biggest commercial ships. Oil is poured into a tanker's hold, and upon arriving at the tanker's destination, the oil is sucked out by machines. Oil tanker crews sometimes use bicycles in order to move quickly from one part of the ship's huge deck to another.

While oil tankers are basic to our nation's economy, cruisers, destroyers, and warships are needed to protect our country. Some cruisers have nuclear engines and carry missiles. Destroyers are smaller than cruisers and can move about more quickly. Aircraft carriers are the biggest warships. Airplanes can take off and land on their decks.

Passenger ships called liners were once the easiest means for people to cross the sea. Today, busy travelers save time by flying. Most liners now are used for vacation cruises. They are like luxury hotels, with restaurants, pools, game rooms, live entertainment, and movies.

The *Queen Mary* was one of the finest transatlantic liners of all time. It is preserved at a dock in Long Beach, California. The *Queen Elizabeth 2* still makes Atlantic crossings, carrying passengers leisurely to their destinations.

Supertankers like this one that carry oil are the largest commercial ships traveling the oceans today.

CHAPTER

AIR TRAVEL

Have you ever wished you could fly like a bird? People have always been interested in things that fly. Artist and inventor Leonardo da Vinci drew pictures of flying machines in the 1500s, but the means to build them did not exist.

In Paris in 1783, Frenchman Joseph Montgolfier built the first hot-air balloon that could carry people suspended in a basket. He and his brother were the first passengers. Later, other people flew in balloons, and hot-air ballooning is still a hobby enjoyed by many people today.

Sir George Cayley was determined to solve the riddle of human flight. In the late 1700s, he worked in a home laboratory where he studied aerodynamics and mechanics. After experimenting with materials and designs, he flew in his first model glider in 1804. It was as big as an airplane but it had no engine. Other inventors improved on his glider, and today pilots fly them on fast, exciting rides.

Frenchman Joseph Montgolfier's hot-air balloon of 1783

39

THE WORLD'S FIRST AIRPLANE

Hot-air balloons and gliders fascinated Orville and Wilbur Wright when they were children. They also liked to make toy helicopters. As men, they built bicycles for a living, but creating flying machines was their hobby. They attached propellers and an engine to a glider and called it a flyer. In 1903, Orville flew their flyer for twelve seconds in the world's first airplane flight.

Many early airplanes had two sets of wings that let them make sharp turns and rolls. In World War I (1914–1918), pilots engaged in shooting battles called biplane maneuvers, or dogfights. Such dogfights marked the beginning of air fighting.

Also in the early 1900s, engineer Igor Sikorsky tried to build a helicopter. When his first attempts failed, he turned to working on airplane designs, but his interest in helicopters remained. In 1939, he built the first American helicopter. It could fly straight up or down, forward or backward, or side to side. It also could stand still in the air. Today, helicopters have many uses in times of both peace and war.

AIRLINERS

In the early 1930s, many Americans began flying in airplanes. Planes were getting bigger and they could fly faster and farther. Seaplanes could even land on water. Passenger planes took on sleek designs similar to today's airliners.

The Boeing 247, launched in 1933, was the first modern airliner. After takeoff, its wheels folded up into the wings, letting it slip easily through the air.

In a daring solo flight in 1927, Charles Lindbergh flew across the Atlantic Ocean, from New York to a hero's welcome in Paris. His plane, *The Spirit of St. Louis,* is on display in Washington D.C.'s Smithsonian Institution.

Five years after Lindbergh's historic flight, Amelia Earhart was the first woman to fly alone across the Atlantic. While attempting to circle the globe in 1937, Earhart's plane was lost. Her disappearance remains a mystery.

Charles Lindbergh poses next to *The Spirit of St. Louis.*

Another of America's first modern planes was the DC-3. It could fly 180 miles per hour and carry twenty-one people.

Rotary engines and propellers powered planes until a German company produced jet engines. In jet planes, a fan sucks air into the front of the engine. Burning engine fuel releases compressed gases under great pressure. These gases exit through the engine's back, thrusting the plane forward.

Jet engines allowed planes to go even faster and farther. There are many kinds of jet planes, and the 747-400 and the 777 are two of the best known. In 1991, newly developed F-117A stealth fighter-bombers helped the United States and its allies win

Most pilots try to avoid storms. But pilots in the 53rd Weather Reconnaissance Squadron fly directly into them.

Their mission: to seek hurricanes and send life-saving data to the U.S. Weather Bureau. Hurricane Hunters fly into a storm and report wind speed data every thirty seconds. This information tells the strength of a storm and where it may hit land. Since 1947, thanks to these Hurricane Hunters, the Weather Bureau has been able to send around-the-clock hurricane warnings to the media. When people hear that a storm may make landfall in their area, they are well advised to take cover.

The Hurricane Hunters' current home is Keesler Air Force Base in Biloxi, Mississippi. These flyers pride themselves on having flown over 100,000 accident-free hours.

the Persian Gulf War. These planes were built with curved or angular surfaces made of special materials that reduced radar reflection and allowed the planes to approach their targets without detection.

SUPERSONIC JETS

In time, engineers developed supersonic jet planes that travel faster than sound. The *Concorde*, a supersonic jet, is today's fastest commercial plane. It was unveiled in 1967 and today it is the world's only supersonic passenger jet. Unfortunately, a crash in 2000 grounded all *Concordes* until the investigation into the cause of the crash is completed.

THE FUTURE OF AIR TRANSPORTATION

In 1957, the Soviet Union launched the first space satellite, *Sputnik*, and the race to explore space began. In 1961, Alan Shepard was the first American launched into space. A year later, John Glenn was the first American to orbit the Earth. Seven years after that, astronauts Neil Armstrong and Edwin Aldrin Jr. walked on the moon.

Although astronauts now live aboard space stations that are orbiting the Earth, it will probably be years before average citizens can travel into outer space. Nevertheless, if you would like to visit a distant planet and see an asteroid up close, someday it may be possible.

Supersonic jets like the *Concorde* are the fastest way to travel a great distance. Until they have once again been determined safe, however, people have to rely on regular jet planes.

For now, those aboard the space shuttle are astronauts working as research scientists. How long will it be before vehicles similar to these are used by ordinary citizens to travel to space?

People working in the land, sea, and air transportation fields often conduct business and measure success by using things like concrete and steel. Yet transportation is really about something more vital: people. No matter how complex our various means of transportation become, the final goal is getting people and the things we produce quickly and safely from here to there.

Chronology

1825	The Erie Canal is completed.
1826	The first horse-drawn train is in operation.
1829	A steam locomotive is used to pull a train.
1869	The transcontinental railroad is completed on May 10.
1877	The internal combustion engine is developed.
1903	Wilbur and Orville Wright fly their first airplane.
1904	The American Automobile Association is organized to help and to protect motorists.
1908	The first Model T Ford comes off the assembly line.
1912	The *Titanic* sinks on its maiden voyage.
1916	Congress passes the Federal Aid Road Act.
1927	Charles Lindbergh flies solo across the Atlantic Ocean.
1932	Amelia Earhart is the first woman to fly solo across the Atlantic Ocean.
1933	Boeing launches the first modern airliner.
1944	Congress approves the Interstate Highway System.
1957	The Soviet Union launches *Sputnik,* the first space satellite.
1961	Alan Shepard is the first American launched into space.
1962	John Glenn is the first American to orbit the Earth.
1969	Men walk on the moon.
1971	Amtrak is created by the Department of Transportation and railroad officials.
1995	Congress passes the National Highway System Designation Act.
2000	The International Space Station is launched.

For Further Information

Books:

Ambrose, Stephen E. *Nothing Like It in the World: The Men Who Built the Transcontinental Railroad 1863–1869*. New York: Simon and Schuster, 2000.

Chant, Christopher. *The Marshall Cavendish Illustrated Guide to Sailing Ships.* Long Island, NY: Marshall Cavendish, 1989.

Chant, Christopher. *The Marshall Cavendish Illustrated Guide to Steamships.* Long Island, NY: Marshall Cavendish, 1989.

Kerrod, Robin. *Amazing Flying Machines*. New York: Knopf, 1992.

Roberts, David. *The Great Book of Railways*. Windermere, FL: Rourke Publishing, 1981.

Stein, Conrad. *The Golden Spike*. Chicago: Children's Press, 1978.

Vogt, Gregory. *Space Stations*. Mankato, MN: Bridgestone Books, Capstone Press, 1999.

Places to Visit:

California State Railroad Museum
101 I Street
Sacramento, CA 95814
www.csrmf.org

Mystic Seaport
The Museum of America
 and the Sea
75 Greenmanville Ave.
Mystic, CT 06355
www.mysticseaport.org

NASA Headquarters
300 E Street, S.W.
Washington, D.C. 20546
www.nasa.gov

National Canal Museum
30 Centre Square
Easton, PA 18042
E-mail ncm@canals.org
www.canals.org

Smithsonian Institution
7th Street and Independence Ave., S.W.
Washington, D.C. 20560
www.smithsonian.com

Other Web Sites to Visit:

Amtrak
www.amtrak.com
Hurricane Hunters
www.hurricanehunters.com

46

Index